Isms

by Kenn Kingt

To

____

From

____

ISMS by Kenn Kington

www.ellieclaire.com

Design by: Jeff & Lisa Franke
Illustrated by: Gregory A. Scott
Photography by: Michael Gomez

For more information contact:
KENN Productions, Inc.
www.kennkington.com
1-888-550-KENN

ISBN 978-1-934770-43-6
Printed in the Untied States of America

Acknowledgements

I want to make sure I do not miss anyone here. So thank YOU! If you are reading this then you are now a personal supporter of the ISMS world. Thank you for enjoying them and thank you for the ISMS you will hear and share and might even take the time to send in and multiply the joy they provide.

Thank you to everyone who speaks or listens or reads...
You too are part of this phenomenon whether you like it or not.

Specific thanks have to go to my wife, Heather, for helping me notice this area of life I just let slip by until I met her.

Special thanks to my fellow comedians and friends Tim and Todd Hawkins who share my enjoyment of this ISMS world and have contributed several that you will read in this book. Also, special thanks to my friends Dee Dee, Jennifer, and Lorrie who edited this to make it look decent. Any mistakes are directly due to my failure to correct them.

Thanks to the hundreds if not thousands of you who take the time after shows and through e-mail to share your ISMS with me. Not all of them are usable in the general public but they are funny because they actually happened!

I think that covers everyone so turn the page and enter the hilarious world of mixed-up, funny and stupid phrases people have actually said...

Introduction

While running together one day with my soon-to-be wife, I noticed something odd. Here is this beautiful woman who finished college with a 4.0 grade point average and she said something a little odd. "I am sweating like a bullet!" I smiled and laughed a little under my breath. She immediately asked what was funny and I replied, "I don't think bullets sweat."

Her response was quite emphatic and clear, "It's a saying!"

Not really! I tried to explain what she said was not the saying at all and "HeatherISMS" were born. I know she is not the first or the only creator of this phenomenon. Over the past decade they have popped up all over the place and I too have even let one or two slip out. The key is that when people say ISMS it fools their minds into thinking it is normal. Thus, they do not hear the conflict in their heads. It takes a "friend" to point it out or clarify this misspeak. Or, in my case, just remember it and share it with thousands of people from the stage during a comedy show.

Enjoy this simple reading and consider being a part of the craze. Just listen. The next time you hear something that just doesn't sound quite right…write it down and send it to me. The next issue of my newsletter or update on my website might just be your comedy writing debut.

Running with my fiancé, Heather, was the first time I ever took notice of what are now known as ISMS. After finishing a workout she proclaimed…

"I am sweating LIKE a bullet."

I am not sure bullets sweat!

Origin: "I am sweating bullets."

A friend, sharing how well his new entrepreneurial efforts were going, told of how hard he had always worked, but now...

"I can finally taste some of the FRUIT at the end of the tunnel."

Maybe that's what that light was all along... Fruit! That "daylight/ train" theory is just a hoax.

Origin: "Light at the end of the tunnel," or "Taste the fruit of our labor."

A woman came up to me at a conference where I had performed and asked if it was difficult to stay in hotels all the time. She shared how she just had to have some kind of ambient noise. Then she added…

"I always bring a small OVULATING fan. Would you like to see it?"

No, I really, specifically, DO NOT want to see it!

Origin: There is such a thing as an "oscillating fan."

While having a rather heated discussion about our checkbook and the always-lacking funds, my wife just blurted out…

"Well, you can't milk a dead horse!"

How do you argue with that?

Origin: "Am I beating a dead horse?" or "You can't milk a dead cow."

I had just finished a show in Montgomery, Alabama, and discovered I had a flat tire. The car was up on the jack and the tire was lying on the ground with a big flat spot. A security guard stopped by, flashed a light on the flat tire and made the obvious statement, "So you got a flat!" Before I could reply he continued…

"Yep, that's flat as a doorknob!"

It was all I could do not to reply, "I guess that makes you 'dumb as a pancake'?"

Origin: "Flat as a pancake," or "Dumb as a doorknob."

I often catch the overnight flight back from a city to be home in the morning. It threw my wife off when I informed her I was not leaving until the next morning. She asked...

"Oh, you couldn't catch the JEDI flight?"

No, I don't think Han Solo is doing that one anymore. Kind of hard to find a good Wookiee co-pilot these days.

A friend moved south and was adjusting quite well. One of his northern friends called to see how it was going and asked...

"What's it like living below the WINN DIXIE line?"

He either needs to go grocery shopping more often or take a history class or BOTH!

Origin: The Mason-Dixon Line is the historical marker to which he was referring.

Another great argument-ender from
my wonderful wife…

"You better watch out or you're going to be up a tree without a paddle."

Why would I need a paddle in the tree?
Are there some mutant squirrels I am not aware of?

Origin: "Up a creek without a paddle," or "Up a tree."

Trying to explain the best option, she said…

"You know a bird in the hand is better than two in a CAGE."

No, not really!

Origin: „Bird in the hand is better than two in the BUSH."

Sometimes we should just be silent. This man was so eager to agree he jumped into the conversation and proclaimed…

"Boy, you hit the TAIL on the MONEY!"

Exactly which end of the money is the tail?

Origin: "Hit the nail on the head," or "You are right on the money."

One guy wrote to me about his father watching a special on PBS. His dad explained how great this hour-long documentary was. When asked what the topic was, his dad explained...

"It is all about the Loch Ness LOBSTER."

Maybe he was dozing off during the show.

Origin: "Loch Ness monster."

Salesmen are the best. I asked how popular this particular car was and he said...

"These things are selling like WILD FLOWERS."

I did not realize people were trying to sell wild flowers. Most people just stop and pick them by the road...

Origin: "Selling like hot cakes," or "Spreading like wild flowers."

Trying to establish the intensity of the moment, he said ...

"If that doesn't rattle your wood, your cage is wet!"

Who make cages out of wood? Why is it wet? If you saw a wooden cage, would you have the uncontrollable urge to shake it?

Origin: "That will rattle you," or "If that doesn't start your fire, your wood is wet."

Attempting to accuse her husband of a similar offense, she clearly stated...

"Well, that is just like the CAT calling the kettle black!"

Why is there a cat on the stove in the first place?

Origin: "The POT calling the kettle black."
We have no idea where the cat came from.

I was looking for a particular item that was hard to find when a friend offered…

"I'll keep my ears posted."

What good is that going to do? I guess I could keep my feet informed?

Origin: "I'll keep my eyes peeled."

WWNCAACDCDDE
1st Annual

During an interview, an applicant was asked,
"What is the best characteristic you bring to the position?"
Her response...

"I am very communicable."

She did NOT get the job and was asked to not breathe on anyone.

Origin: We think she was trying to say she communicated well. Obviously, not so much.

We were with some friends talking about what a friend really is when my bride proclaims…

"I am a great friend!
I'm as LOYAL as a
heart attack."

I don't think I want you to be my friend.

Origin: "Serious as a heart attack," or "Loyal as the day is long."

Observing a gentleman that might be a workaholic, this guy said…

"He's working both sides of the CANDLE."

A brilliant observation! Now go back and lie down and think of other brilliant things to say.

Origin: "Working both sides of the street," or "Burning the candle at both ends."

A gentleman, cautioning his friend not
to be too anxious, advised...

"Don't put your CHICKEN in front of the horse."

That might actually be what motivated
the chicken to cross the road.

Origin: "Don't put the CART before the horse."
I am not sure how the chicken enters the picture.

While performing at the state fair in Missouri, I was offered a quick bite to eat in the hospitality tent and was given some interesting condiment options for my hotdog. The helpful young lady inquired…

"Would you like mustard or nothing or BOTH."

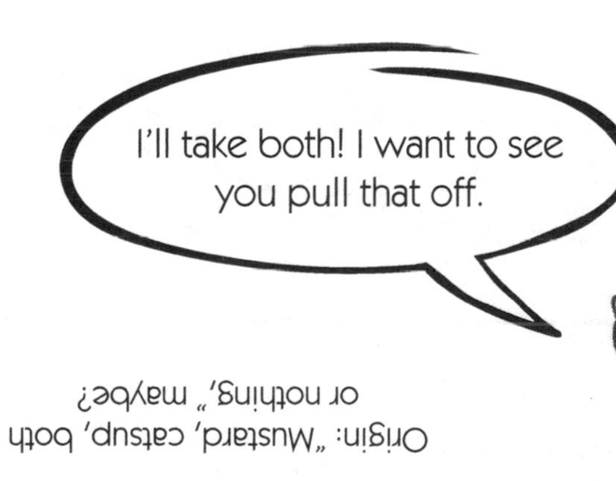

I'll take both! I want to see you pull that off.

Origin: "Mustard, catsup, both or nothing," maybe?

A football coach was asked about an especially difficult opponent that his team faced later in the season and proclaimed...

"We'll tackle that bridge when we get to it."

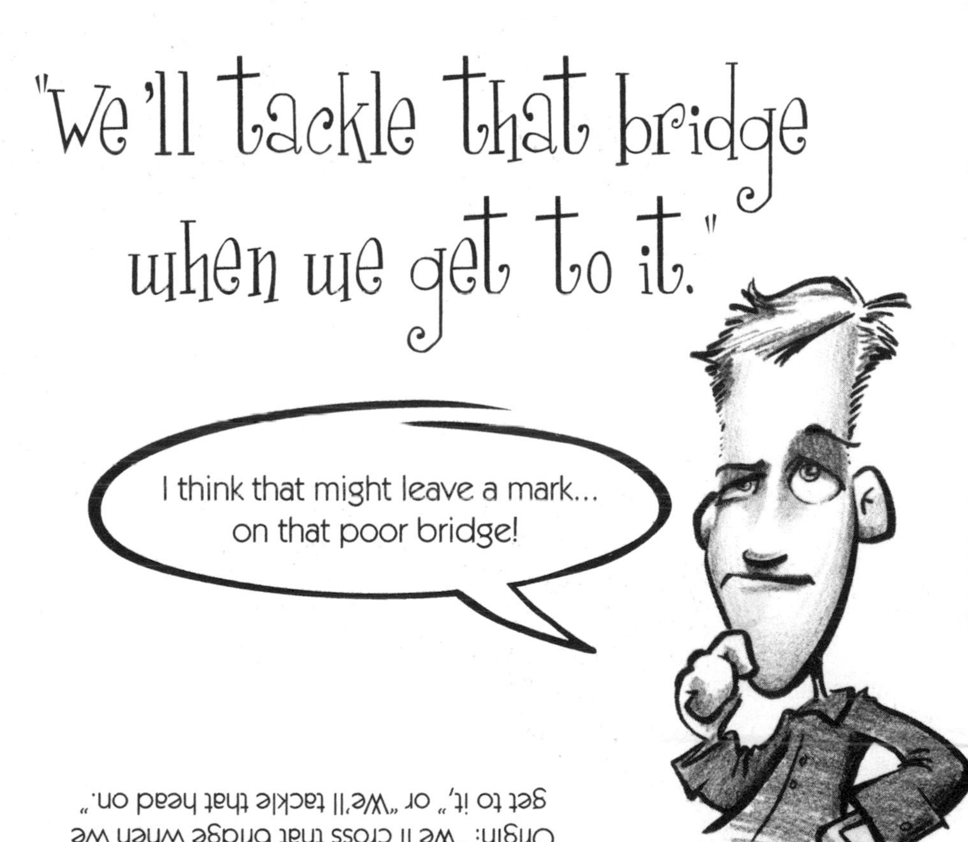

I think that might leave a mark...
on that poor bridge!

Origin: "We'll cross that bridge when we get to it," or "We'll tackle that head on."

I overheard a secretary validating her friend on the phone by saying...

"You can lead a horse to water, but that doesn't make it right!"

I just don't see the conflict in letting a horse drink water.

Origin: "Lead a horse to water, but you can't make him drink," or "Even if others do it, that doesn't make it right."

I passed an unhappy customer in the mall who obviously felt slighted by a salesman. She angrily questioned…

"How do you sleep with yourself?"

Well…I go to bed…
and there I am!

Origin: "How do you sleep at night?" or "How do you live with yourself?"

Heather and I were shopping for a new mini van and we had narrowed it down to two. I asked which she liked best...

"It's just six of one or a DOZEN of another."

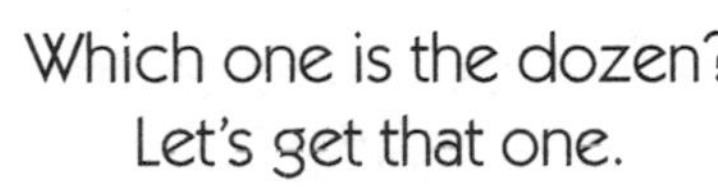

Which one is the dozen?
Let's get that one.

Origin: "Six of one; a half-dozen of another."

It runs in the family…
My wife's father was explaining an alternative way to accomplish the same task and stated…

"Well, whatever TURNS your boat."

Would that be a rudder?
He said, "Yes, exactly. That is why it's a saying."
I cannot win.

Origin: "Whatever FLOATS your boat."

A friend was talking about persevering and staying to the very end. His analogy was a bit unusual when he advised...

"The CONDUCTOR has to go down with the TRAIN."

If he sinks a train, he is doing something seriously wrong.

Origin: "The captain has to go down with the ship."

One woman describing the struggles of another couple to her friend…

"Her poor husband is treating her like eggshells."

Does that mean he is throwing her away or being very gentle with her?

Origin: "Walking on eggshells," or "Treating her like dirt."

Using her great discernment skills in the awkward situation, she accused…

"I smell a FISH!"

The rat is finally off the hook.

Origin: "I smell a RAT."

My brother had a date with a young lady who had an interview the next day. He asked if she was prepared. She confidently replied...

"I think I have all my eggs in a row."

Were those duck eggs?
I guess lining up eggs shows organizational skills.

Origin: "I have all my eggs in one basket," or "I have all my ducks in a row."

My friend was struggling to find a new job. My wife commented about his aptitude…

"He is not the sharpest COOKIE in the shed."

Apparently that is where we are keeping the cookies now.

Origin: "Sharpest tool in the shed."

One girl was laughing when she shared how her friend just did not get it when she said…

"He is just a FOX in WOLF'S clothing."

Then he is not a real smart fox is he?

Origin: "A wolf in sheep's clothing."

This same girl followed that revelation with her own attempt to explain it…

"You know, it is supposed to be 'SHEEP in WOLF'S clothing'!"

Do two wrongs make a right?

Origin: Again, "A wolf in sheep's clothing."

At the weekly meetings, the boss starts with the same statement every week: "You all know why we have this meeting..."

"It is to make sure we have all our DUCKS on the same page."

Why do people struggle so much with this duck thing?

Origin: "Make sure we are all on the same PAGE."
Ducks have NOTHING to do with it.

Another boss had a similar statement
to start each meeting...

"We want to make sure we are on the same PLATE."

Maybe he was raised in a large family
and had to share.

Origin: Again, "Make sure we are all on the same PAGE."

Sometimes a sermon is so moving and life changing you want to pass it on to others.

"You have to get the tape of that sermon. I was glued to the ceiling."

I guess the balcony just wasn't high enough for some reason.

Origin: "Scrape me off the ceiling," or "I was glued to the edge of my seat."

A friend was driving with his wife and passed a billboard advertising a festival in the northern part of the state called Oktoberfest. She actually asked…

"I wonder when Oktoberfest is?"

I'm going out on a limb here and say... OCTOBER?

Origin: When the name of a month is in the name of the event, go with that month.

In an attempt to warn a fellow staff member of a talkative woman in the congregation, the pastor shared...

"She is nice, but she will talk your ARMS off."

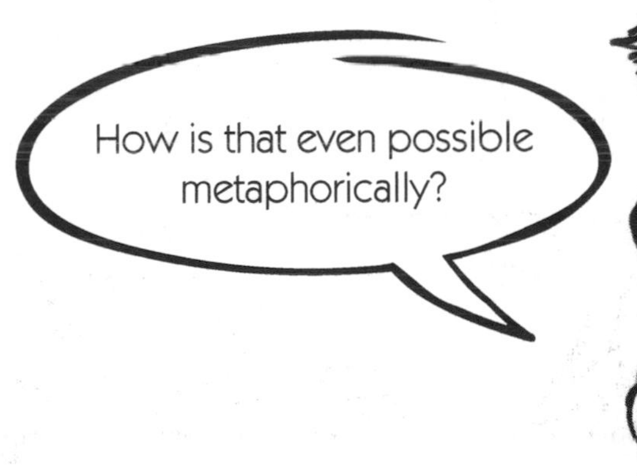
How is that even possible metaphorically?

Origin: "Talk your EARS off."

Our kids were asking for some money for something frivolous and my wife asked…

"Do you think money grows under ROCKS?"

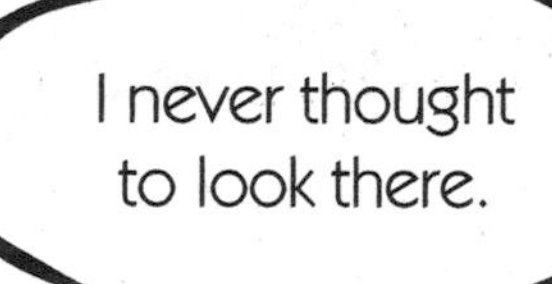
I never thought to look there.

Origin: „Do you think money grows on TREES?"

Sitting in church one Sunday I heard the announcement for an event that had already happened. The man giving the annoucements caught the mistake and said...

"Wait a minute... that's water OVER the bridge."

Isn't "water over the bridge" a FLOOD?

Origin: "Water under the bridge," or "Water over the dam."

Walking by a youth soccer field I overheard a frustrated coach yell at a group of 4 year olds...

"Quit running around like a bunch of chickens with your LEGS cut off!"

Those must be some talented chickens.

Origin: "Running around like a chicken with its HEAD cut off."

Two women gossiping about a much younger acquaintance marrying a much older, richer man deduced...

"She is just a GRAVE digger."

Maybe he can get a discount from her when he kicks the bucket.

Origin: "She is a GOLD digger."

A lady was trying to teach appreciation, and got a little confused…

"Don't KISS a gift horse in the mouth."

My advice: "Don't kiss any horse in the mouth or anywhere for that matter."

Origin: "Don't LOOK a gift horse in the mouth."

During a round of golf, I asked my friend about his college days. He said in an embarrassed tone, "I don't like to talk about it..."

"I have a lot of BLACK SHEEP in my closet."

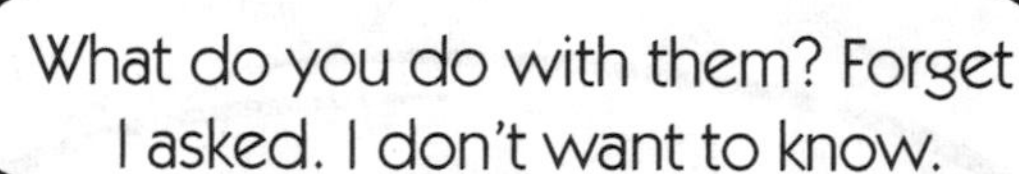

What do you do with them? Forget I asked. I don't want to know.

Origin: "I am the black sheep of the family," or "I have skeletons in my closet."

She was very proud of her victory
and proclaimed…

"Put that in your
little red wagon
and smoke it."

I tried but could not get the wagon lit.

Origin: "Put that in your PIPE and smoke it," or "Put that in your little red wagon" (no smoking required).

The CEO of a company was recapping the year and explaining how some results could have been better, but...

"Hindsight is 50/50."

Hindsight must be a bit fuzzy, too.

Origin: "Hindsight is 20/20."

The head basketball coach at a Division 1 program was frustrated with his players and out of his frustration screamed…

"Come on people, this is not ROCKET surgery!"

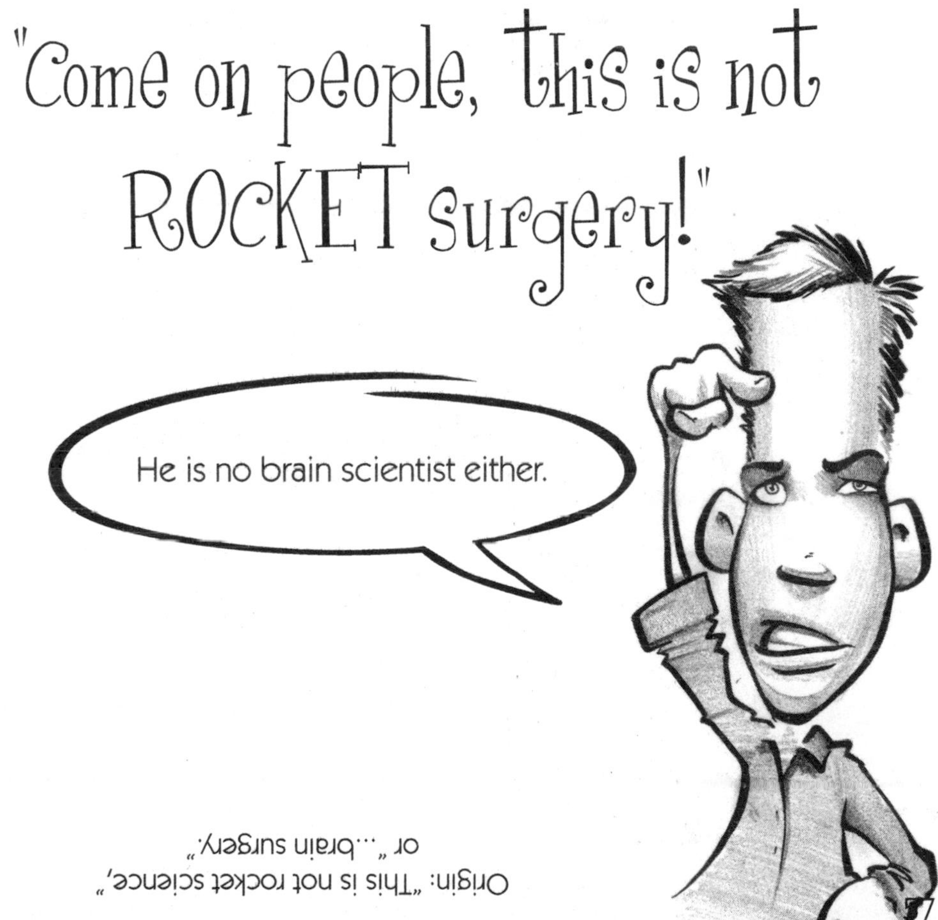
He is no brain scientist either.

Origin: "This is not rocket science,"
or "…brain surgery."

Explaining the futility of the situation,
this lady proclaimed...

"You can't teach a DEAD dog new tricks."

However, he is really good at playing dead!

Origin: "You can't teach an OLD dog new tricks."

The president of a company was forecasting a bright future after a trying year, but said optimistically…

"If we keep working hard, I really feel our business is just going to BOOMERANG."

My advice is to sell the company halfway into the year.

Origin: "The business is going to skyrocket," or "…going to boom."

Salesmen are the best for these. After a long negotiation, he tried to find that common ground to make the deal work.

"I think we are almost there. We just have to find a way to see TOE to TOE."

I am not sure that is physically possible... No deal!

Origin: "Go toe to toe," or "See eye to eye."

Facing a tough decision, my friend
came to the conclusion…

"I am just going to have to bite the BUBBLE."

Does the taste distract
from the pain?

Origin: "Bite the BULLET."

Trying to soften the frustration of making a mistake, this friend made it even more thwarting with his offering of...

"You know what they say, two birds are better than a dog barking up the wrong tree."

Who exactly says that?

Origin: "A bird in hand is better than two in the bush," or "A dog barking up the wrong tree."

Staff meetings are such fertile ground for ISMS to flow from the mouths of leaders, especially when a tough decision needs to be made. This pastor just had to interject...

"Well, I think we ought to bite while the worm is hot!"

Is this Jr. High ministry?

Origin: "Strike while the iron is hot," or "The early bird gets the worm."

Gossip often produces some really good ISMS. Wishing she could get in on what happened behind closed doors, she said…

"I would love to be a fly IN the wall."

I am not sure what good that would do. It is hard to hear while encased in drywall.

Origin: "A fly ON the wall."

Explaining the futility of the situation, this lady proclaimed…

"Do you think I am just CONCEIVING myself?"

I've never seen someone conceive themselves, but I think you would know.

We used to call them "Heatherisms"
because of questions like this:
Heather (my wife) asked me once...

"Do you think I am just dragging a dead dog into the ground?"

Why would you try to walk a dead dog in the first place?

Origin: "Beat a dead horse," or "Run it into the ground."

A waitress once apologized for the trainee who was waiting on our table by wispering…

"She is still GREEN behind the ears."

Should she see a doctor about that or is she a distant relative of Aquaman?

Origin: "She is WET behind the ears," or "She is still green."

TEXAS
TNT

While driving by a perfect piece of real estate with a dilapidated home sitting on it, we noticed an older gentleman there who was probably the owner. My friend made the insightful comment...

"He probably doesn't realize he's sitting on a LAND mine."

Should we stop and save him?
His next step could be his last!

Origin: "Sitting on a GOLD mine."

We can all be forgetful. What we choose to do when that happens is another issue…

"I drew a total BLOCK."

I am going to try that. When I forget, I just pick up a pencil and start sketching…

Origin: "I drew a total BLANK."

Perspective is important. After making it through a very rough time, my friend observed...

"She has a new LEASH on life."

Origin: "A new LEASE on life."

A shy woman came up after a show and told me how she did not like crowds or attention. She could not figure out why I laughed when she said...

"I would like to remain UNANIMOUS."

It is going to be hard to get everyone to agree with you if you do not like being around them.

Origin: "I like to be ANONYMOUS."

The manager was trying to reduce the number of costly mistakes but was making it more painful than necessary by saying…

"We have to quit STABBING ourselves in the foot."

If you are out of bullets that might be your only option.

Origin: "Quit SHOOTING ourselves in the foot."

While updating their daughter who was away at college, the father explained, "Your mom has been taking one of those first aid courses. That way..."

"If I ever choke on something, she can do that HEMLOCK maneuver."

I guess in that family they do not help you, they poison you and end it even faster!

Origin: "The Heimlich maneuver."

A proud father once gazed at his son with pride and shared with me...

"He's got the WORLD by the seat of HIS pants."

I am still not sure what that means, but it was a proud moment.

Origin: "He is flying by the seat of his pants," or "He has the world in the palm of his hand."

My wife has a great sense of discernment,
if not a clear way to communicate...

"That guy is trying to pull the wool over your SHOULDERS."

Is he trying to deceive me or
just help me keep warm?

Origin: "Pull the wool over your EYES."

After a short night's sleep my friend's wife asked him how he had slept. He quickly shot back...

"I slept like a bird."

You were on a wire somewhere?

Origin: "Eat like a bird,"
or "Sleep like a log."

I made the observation to a friend one night that he looked spent. His reply...

"Yeah man, I am as tired as a doorknob."

To this day I have no idea what that means.

Origin: I just said... to this day I have no idea what that means.

We have very short arguments because of statements like this...

"You are treading in hot water!"

Honey, that's a Jacuzzi!
I don't mind being there!

Origin: "In hot water," or "Skating on thin ice."

I wish I had more time with my grandparents. They are gone now, but a friend shared as ISM from his grandfather that is exactly what ISMS are all about.

"Who let the cat out of the barn?"

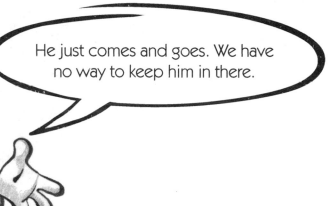

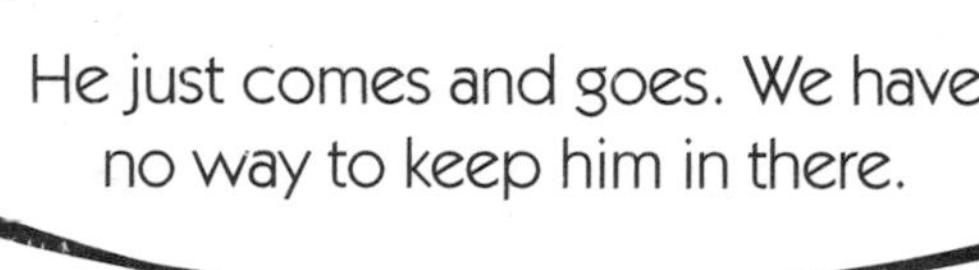

He just comes and goes. We have no way to keep him in there.

Origin: "Let the cat out of the bag," or "...horse out of the barn."

This college student had been up all night studying and felt good about his knowledge...

"I know this stuff like the back of my HEAD."

Take a mirror to the test and you should be fine.

Origin: "I know this like the back of my HAND."

On our trip home from the beach, Heather was trying to get our two-year-old to take a nap. She sang to her softly…

"Jesus loves me this I know.
For the Bible tells me so.
Up above the world so high
like a diamond in the sky."

Then she looked at me and asked, "What's the next line?"
I said, "Q, R, S... T, U, V..."

Origin: Apparently, most children's songs are sung to a very similar tune.

One of the most recent ISMS happened at the pool in our neighborhood. The head of the pool committee wanted some input on how to keep non-residents from using the pool and asked what should go on the sign to be posted on the gate. Heather chimed right in and I thought, here it comes. She said, "Be simple and firm…"

"Trespassers will be violated!"

That would certainly work, but I'm not sure we can do that legally.

Origin: "Trespassers will be PROSECUTED."

S.S.Mirage

After a couple of months of searching, my friend had still not found a new job. My compassionate wife made it clear: "If he does not get his act together..."

"He is going to be up a creek without WATER!"

I suppose the paddle is pretty much useless at that point. Plus, I forgot and left it in the tree.

Origin: "Up a creek without a PADDLE."

Nervous about the upcoming interview,
the candidate confided...

"I am not sure I can cut the CHEESE."

Origin: "Cut the MUSTARD."

The guys in the office were all talking football when the attractive new bride of a co-worker walked through the office. One sports genius commented...

"He has definitely out-punted his woman!"

If you cannot kick a ball farther than your wife can, you should not be allowed to watch football.

Origin: The football term is "He out-kicked his coverage."

Rationalizing can often breed ISMS. Deciding not to do a mail-out but instead inform the people by having the members take it to the community, this pastor felt good about his decision...

"Mouth to mouth really is the best advertising."

What denomination are you guys?

Origin: "Word of mouth."

My friend's wife was chastening him about his bad attitude and strongly recommended...

"You better get that chip off your BACKSIDE!"

I didn't know it was back there.

Origin: "Chip off your SHOULDER."

WAR
AND
PEACE

After a rough period of time, the worn out soul made the plea...

"I just need some time to DECOMPOSE."

You can do that when you're dead.
Try a few days vacation for now.

Origin: "I need time to DECOMPRESS."

Only in a church staff meeting can such a multiple concoction of mixed-up phrases happen so eloquently. The pastor's evaluation of a certain individual was…

"He's bright as a whip and dumb as a tack."

When you can mix up four or more sayings, it is in the category of BRILLIANT ISMS!

Origin: "Sharp as a tack," "Smart as a whip," "Dumb as a doorknob," or "Not the brightest bulb in the chandelier."